ID# THE MIRACLE OF MARRIAGE

by Bill & Margaret Panko

THE MIRACLE OF MARRIAGE

ISBN 1-885342-00-4   US $3.95   Canada $4.95
Copyrighted © July 31, 1993 - Bill & Margaret Panko

ALL RIGHTS RESERVED. Reproduction in whole or part without written permission **and** verbal consent is strictly prohibited. Violators will **be** prosecuted to the FULL extent of the spiritual and natural law.

All scripture quotations are derived from the King James version of the bible.

Book designed, produced and published by:
CREATIVE WAYS
509 Marie Drive
South Holland, Illinois 60473

Cover photography by:
KEISMAN & KEISMAN
2211 Hermon Lane
Zion, Illinois 60099

Printed by:
LITHO COLOR PRESS
9816 W. Roosevelt Road
Westchester, Illinois 60153

The Miracle of Marriage

by Bill & Margaret Panko

DEDICATION

This prophetic marriage ceremony is dedicated to the Dual Divine Authors of Prophecy and this written work! I am referring to the Lord Jesus Christ who is the Glorified Expressed Word of Prophecy and the Holy Ghost as the Sublime Spirit of Prophecy!! May these Members of the Triune God **speak** into our lives and **breathe** upon our beings forever! Amen!

THE ORIGIN

THE MIRACLE OF MARRIAGE was created because of a divine dissatisfaction with existing marriage ceremonies. As a couple, we hungered and ached for a revelatory service straight from the Source that revealed God's original intention for this holy covenant, and focused on what the Trinity wanted to accomplish in our lives. The form was a result of a compulsion for proper, puritanical marital order and a necessity for a foundation established upon anointed apostolic and prophetic ministry. It was written because of an obsession to understand the reality and significance of marriage, as well as an intense yearning to be joined and united with Jesus Christ in His forthcoming return. And finally, it was published to present the spiritual seriousness of marriage to all believers in accordance with the Word of God and the genuine Church of the Lord Jesus Christ!

FOREWORD

I am confident that this God- breathed revelation will greatly **influence** and drastically **revolutionize** the cumulative Body of Christ! It will **illuminate** the global community to the sanctity of marriage as a sacrament ordained by the Godhead. It will **inform** the corporate company to the real purpose and meaning of holy matrimony. And it will **reform** the way the union of man and woman is perceived, believed and daily experienced by saints!

The order of service will **reveal** the spiritual significance of the conjugal covenant and its natural importance, and serve as a basis for daily application. If this rite is **observed, adhered to and employed** as a guideline for your marriage ceremony, the unifying and uniting of two believers will **ascend** to new spiritual dimensions and transcendental heights to eventually arrive at the supernatural, which is heaven's original intention for marriage.

Furthermore, I am absolutely certain that this book will **enlighten** the five-fold governmental officers in the body to the manifold miraculous power available in a Godly relationship, and the unlimited grace that is supernaturally activated and released in the nuptial agreement. This unstoppable spiritual force is granted by the Trinity **ONLY** in the celestial covenant of marriage, for **dynamic and overcoming team ministry!** So it is written, so let it be done!

THE ORDER OF SERVICE

* INVOCATION AND ADDRESSING OF FAMILIES - Attending Pastor   1
* CEREMONIAL PROCESSION - Keyboards and trumpet   1
* INTRODUCTION OF GROOM - Master of Ceremonies   1
* INTRODUCTION OF BRIDE - Master of Ceremonies   4
* MINISTERIAL VOWS - Ceremonial Celebrant   6
* CHARGE TO THE BRIDE & GROOM - Ceremonial Celebrant   8
* THE ORIGIN OF MAN, WOMAN AND MARRIAGE   9
* CONFESSION OF CHRIST AND PROFESSION OF FAITH   11
* VOWS TO WITNESSES   14
* SERMON - *"The Miracle of Marriage"* - Ceremonial Celebrant   15
* PUBLIC PROFESSION OF VOWS - Ceremonial Celebrant   15
* THE RING SERVICE - Ceremonial Celebrant   19
* HONORING OF BRIDE & GROOM - Bride and Groom   22

* LIGHTING OF THE UNITY CANDLE - Bride, Groom and Ceremonial Celebrant 22

* PARTAKING OF HOLY COMMUNION - Bride, Groom and Ceremonial Celebrant 23

* PRONOUNCEMENT OF HOLY UNION - Ceremonial Celebrant 26

* ANOINTING AND BLESSING OF UNION - Ceremonial Celebrant 27

* PROPHETIC PRESBYTERY TO THE BRIDE AND GROOM - Ceremonial Celebrant and other invited ministers 28

* PROPHETIC PRESBYTERY TO THE IMMEDIATE FAMILIES - Ceremonial Celebrant and other invited ministers 28

* PRESENTATION TO THE CONGREGATION OF WITNESSES 29

* THE SERMON 30

* THE HONORING OF BILL PANKO 33

* THE HONORING OF MARGARET PANKO 36

THE MIRACLE OF MARRIAGE

INVOCATION AND ADDRESSING OF FAMILIES - Attending Pastor, *"... and now let us begin The Miracle of Marriage."*

CEREMONIAL PROCESSION - Keyboard & Trumpet

INTRODUCTION OF BRIDE & GROOM - Master of Ceremonies

GROOM'S ENTRANCE: TO THE CONGREGATION - Master of Ceremonies

It is scripturally understood in marriage that the man represents the person of Jesus Christ, who is the head of His earthen, spiritual body. In the beginning, the Lord God initiated the sacrament of marriage as the most sacred spiritual covenant between two human beings. Initially, marriage was patterned after the foreordained spiritual consolidation of Christ and His glorified church. For even as the man is joined unto the woman in wedded union, so will Christ be united with all believers in the miracle of holy matrimony, for eternal spiritual relations and an everlasting coupling of Creator with creation. As the Spiritual Head and His earthen Body renew the conjugal ties of their covenant, the Lord Jesus Christ will be irrevocably united with The Church to co-habit and govern the earth in the New Jerusalem. This shall shortly come to pass.

As it is scribed and recorded in the old testament, the prophet Daniel beheld a preincarnate manifestation of Jesus Christ as the Ancient of Days. As the seer gazed upon His glistening countenance, the oracle was dazzled by the splendid appearance and vesture of the great *"I AM"* which glowed as white as snow. The Anointed One was completely veiled with this glorious, radiating mantle down to His very feet.

In the fullness of times, the Spoken and Written Word of God became flesh and dwelled among men. After His public ministry, death and resurrection,

Jesus Christ ascended to the right hand of God the Father to rule heaven and earth for all eternity. The first century disciples eyewitnessed this translation and watched Jesus disappear into the clouds of heaven. As it was then, so it shall be - NOW!!!!

The Living Word of God shall return to the earth to rapture His church and unite Himself with the corporate body. The bible confirms this in Acts 1:11 for two angels revealed, *"This same Jesus, which is taken up from you into heaven, shall come in like manner as you have seen him ascend into paradise."* This scripture shall shortly be fulfilled. It will be accomplished when the Son of Man is revealed in the clouds of heaven with all authority, power and great glory. At that time, Jesus shall commission and appoint His holy angels to gather up and assemble His elect from one end of the earth to the other. Look up, for the Redeemer draws near.

It is written in 1 Thessalonians 4:16 that *"the Lord himself shall descend from heaven with a shout, with the voice of the archangel and with the great sound of the trumpet of God."* (Trumpeter plays briefly and concludes with a final crescendo) **BEHOLD, THE BRIDEGROOM! COME FORTH TO MEET HIM!** (Slight pause as Groom begins his procession)

The apostle John was spiritually privileged to witness the events that we are currently experiencing and preview the phenomenal developments that are rapidly approaching. The second coming of Christ was disclosed unto this disciple in a heavenly vision which is recorded in Revelation 19:11-16. John documents what he observed and wrote, *"I saw heaven opened, and behold A WHITE HORSE...* **(Stop! Groom makes grand entrance on a white horse, proceeds to altar, dismounts and releases the animal)**

And He that sat upon him was called Faithful and True, and in righteousness doth he judge and make war. His eyes were as a flame of fire, and on his head were many crowns; and he had a name written, that no man knew, but he himself. He was clothed in a vesture dipped in blood; and His name is called THE WORD OF GOD. The armies which were in heaven followed him upon white horses, clothed in fine linen, white and clean. And out of his mouth goeth a sharp sword...And he hath on his vesture and on his thigh a name written: KING OF KINGS AND LORD OF LORDS."

Oh, Church of the Living God, prepare to be joined to the bridegroom in marriage when He comes. Be ready for the approaching marriage feast. Have your lamps filled and burning with oil. For thy husband is thy Maker and the Lord of Hosts is His name.

GROOM: *"SHOW ME THE BRIDE, THE LAMB'S WIFE."*

BRIDE'S ENTRANCE: TO THE CONGREGATION - Master of Ceremonies

It is also a scriptural reality in marriage that the woman represents the genuine, worldwide Church of the Lord Jesus Christ, which is His spiritual body encased in earthen vessels. Under the auspices of the old testament, the marriage ceremony was a type and shadow of the universal unification of Christ and His church. The promise, vow and covenant of eternal espousal spiritually bound the nation of Israel to God. God confirmed this in Hosea 2:19-20 when He declared, *"I will **BETROTH THEE UNTO ME FOREVER**, yea, I will betroth thee unto me in **righteousness**, and in **judgement**, and in **lovingkindness**, and in **mercies**. I will even betroth thee unto me in **faithfulness**."* In this context, betrothal means engagement for marriage. Spiritual matrimony was a mutual pledge and binding contract between Creator and chosen creation, in which both members committed themselves to one another in the bonds of love and devotion.

The marriage of God to Israel was naturally consummated in the new covenant as the prophecies and promises of old were actualized and perfected by Y'shua ha Moshia. Through Jesus the Messiah, God extended his exclusive covenant of love, grace and mercy first unto the Jews and then to all Gentiles. This was done so all nations of the earth could experience intimate relationship and enter into personal covenant with the Almighty God! Halleluia!

The ultimate marriage of Christ and His Church will COMMENCE at the rapture of the company of believers and CONCLUDE at the Marriage Supper of the Lamb. The bible confirms this for *"the dead in Christ shall rise first, then those who remain shall be caught up together with them in the clouds of heaven to meet the Lord in the air."* The marital unification which initially occurs at the great taking away shall culminate at the ultimate Table of the Lord. For then, the body of believers shall be one with the Lord forever! And blessed are they who are called to the Marriage Supper of the Lamb! Amen!!

The translation of Christ's worldwide spiritual Body is a mystery that has been revealed to the church age by the Holy Ghost. The Apostle Paul disclosed this miraculous metamorphosis in 1 Corinthians 15:51-52. It is written, *"We shall not all sleep, but we shall all be changed, In a moment, in the twinkling of an eye, at the last trump: for the trumpet shall sound, and the dead shall be raised incorruptible, and we shall be changed."* Only then shall the bride of

Christ be transfigured in glory and transformed into the image of the Anointed One. For the corruptible body will be clad with incorruption and the mortal being will be shod with immortality. The countenance of the global bride shall radiate like lightning and her raiment shall glisten as snow. The church that is perfected and clothed in glory will rule and reign over the earth with Christ for they have overcome great tribulation and are worthy.

The Church of Christ in heaven is described in the book of Revelation as a *"great multitude, that no man could number, of all nations, and kindreds, and peoples, and tongues, who stood before the throne, and before the Lamb, clothed with white robes. . .Be glad, rejoice and give honor to Jesus: for the Marriage of the Lamb is come, and His wife hath made herself ready...* **BEHOLD, THE BRIDE COMETH!** (Stop! Bride enters in glorious carriage driven by a white horse, exits coach and engaged couple behold and gaze upon each other for the first time)

She is arrayed in fine linen that is clean, white and bright. For the fine linen is the righteousness of the saints." The bride is prepared and adorned as a treasure for her husband. And even as she is espoused only to one man, so the church will be exclusively presented to Jesus as a chaste virgin without spot or wrinkle! Amen! The bride is dressed in white linen signifying her innocence, chastity and virtuousness. She bears the all inclusive color of spotlessness for she has been tried, purified and perfected in the image of Christ.

(Enter Bride's name here and all places indicated hereafter), in the same manner that the bridegroom rejoices over the bride and Jesus rejoices over His church, so the Heavenly Father rejoices over thee. It is written, *"I will greatly rejoice in the Lord and my soul shall be joyful in my God. For He hath clothed me with the garments of salvation and hath covered me with the robe of righteousness, as a bridegroom decketh himself with ornaments, and as a bride adorneth herself with jewels."*

MINISTERIAL VOWS - Ceremonial Celebrant

This day, *(insert date of wedding)*, we are gathered together in the sight of the Triune God, the angels of heaven and this company of witnesses to unite *(name of Bride and Groom)* in the sacred bond of holy matrimony. In the very beginning, God unified man and woman in the spirit as male and female and designated that unctuous union as *"marriage"*. Marriage is God's most honorable spiritual and natural covenant because it represents and personifies the celestial consolidation of Christ and His Church. Therefore, let us with all seriousness invite in the Divine Presence of God and invoke His glory for this special occasion.

I ask that the congregation remain standing as we go before the Lord in prayer. Let the Holy Trinity which consists of God the Father, The Lord Jesus Christ and the Holy Ghost, who bear ALL AUTHORITY, POWER AND DOMINION in heaven and earth, look with great favor and abundant mercy upon this obedient manservant and humble handmaiden, to impart the **supernatural grace** needed for a victorious relationship, a triumphant marriage and a prosperous and flourishing ministry. Father God, grant unto this couple the peace of mind and anointed assurance that they have been brought together by Thy Providence for the fulfillment of Your perfect will in obedience to Christ. This day, let them be eternally joined together by Your Spirit for the continuance of the ministry of Your Son, the profit of people and the advancement of the kingdom of God on the earth. We ask this in Jesus' name. Amen!

We have come together today, to behold and witness the miraculous joining of the devoted LOVE of this couple with the ageless perfect AGAPE of the Godhead by the POWER of the Holy Spirit, who is continuously perfecting *(Bride and Groom)*. They come together before their Creator, myself as a genuine minister of the gospel and these witnesses, to join their spirits, hearts and lives for all eternity. This will be accomplished as they solemnly assert and publicly profess their mutual amour and affection for each other by proclaiming vows. They will pledge their lives to each other for a lifetime of sharing, which includes spiritual and natural service unto each other as unto the Lord.

The verbal expression of their promises will cause the power of God to be activated and A MIRACLE will transpire. This only occurs because words are made of breath and breath contains life. God will employ the breath, life and spirit that is released by *(Bride and Groom)* to permanently bond them together in Christ by their prophetic declaration. The miracle that occurs will involve the unifying, uniting and merging of two separate individuals into one new spirit being by the omnipotence of Almighty God! *(Bride and Groom)* will actually become one new spiritual creature in His sight. And this matrimonial affiliation will be fourfold. They will be joined together **spiritually** by the Triune Being, **soulishly** by the establishment and continual development of a Godly soul tie, **physically** when the marriage is consummated and also **financially.**

Lord Jesus, we give you the praise, honor and glory for this relationship, and for all that they will do in ministry by the power of the Holy Spirit. Let them enter into an inseparable marriage in conjunction with the oneness of You and Your church, and be yoked together in the unanimity of the Godhead. We ask this in your mighty name. Amen! You may be seated.

CHARGE TO THE BRIDE & GROOM - Ceremonial Celebrant

I now charge you both, as you stand in the very presence of God and His glory, to always remember your oaths of love and to faithfully observe your marriage vows. Abide by and comply with the sacred scriptures as the foundation of your personal relationship with your Creator, for the establishment of a successful marriage and the continuance of a blessed home. Keep, obey and incessantly execute the solemn vows you are about to make. Do not be deceived by hearing only, but do, live and fulfill the Word of God! Live the remainder of your earthly existence, first for Jesus as your Lord, and then for each other as your considered neighbor. Conduct your life in passionate charity, vehement selflessness and fervid truth. Never be deceived by God's adversary to believe a lie about each other, the sanctity of marriage or the validity of the bible. So it is spoken, so let it be done.

THE ORIGIN OF MAN, WOMAN AND MARRIAGE - Ceremonial Celebrant

In the beginning, the Lord God formed man of the dust of the ground and breathed into his nostrils the breath of life, which ensouled him as a living, human entity. However, among all the living creatures of the earth, there was not found a suitable mate and compatible counterpart for man. The Lord God recognized this personal need for like human fellowship and caused a deep sleep to fall upon man. As man rested, the Lord took one of the ribs from his side and created a woman. God presented the woman unto the man who exclaimed about the withdrawal from his body and the apportionment of his soul. He prophesied, *"This is now bone of my bones, and flesh of my flesh."* The man called the living human being made in HIS similitude *"woman"* because she was conceived of and taken out of man.

In their original existence, man and woman were created equal. Presently, men and women still remain in the spiritual equivalence and natural parity of their original creation. This is biblically supported by the fact that woman was fashioned and given life from man's side. The woman was not brought into existence to be controlled, dominated or lorded over. Yea rather, she was created, provided to and bestowed upon man as a gift from God. Back then and today, the original purpose of woman was to be a spiritual and natural auxiliary who assists, comforts, supports, encourages and loves man.

Marriage was originally instituted in the lives of the first male and female who were formed in the PROPHETIC NATURE of God. God ordained marriage as a spiritual contract between the two glorified persons created in His image and likeness. Today, the nuptial compact remains in the identical state of its original inception. Marriage is now and will always be a spiritual covenant between two God fearing, regenerate believers! Amen!

When gracious words of inspired life are professed in accordance with the written Word of God between two born-again persons, the **POWER OF GOD** goes into operation. When the power of God is energized, **MIRACLES** are the result. Today, a miracle will take place right before your very eyes as pledges are declared and promises are made. In actuality, a verbal PROPHETIC COVENANT will be established, formed and sealed by the WORDS OF THEIR MOUTH!! This will occur through the release of the breath, life, spirit and faith of these two renewed people. The Heavenly Father will honor their request to become one and will fuse them together in an inseparable spiritual union destined for great power and glory! Halleluia!

CONFESSION OF CHRIST AND PROFESSION OF FAITH - Ceremonial Celebrant

TO THE BRIDE - Ceremonial Celebrant

(Bride's name), have you accepted Jesus Christ as your personal Lord and Savior? *"I have."* Will you consistently and fervently live for Him for the remainder of your natural life? *"I will."* Have you received the Holy Spirit as documented in the second chapter of Acts with the evidence of speaking in other tongues and prophecy? *"I have."* Do you readily accept the call of God upon your life? *"I do."* Have you embraced the ministry for which you were created and are beginning? *"I have."*

TO THE GROOM - Ceremonial Celebrant

(Groom's name), have you accepted Jesus Christ as your personal Lord and Savior? *"I have."* Will you consistently and fervently live for Him for the remainder of your natural life? *"I will."* Have you received the Holy Spirit as documented in the second chapter of Acts with the evidence of speaking in other tongues and prophecy? *"I have."* Do you readily accept the call of God upon your life? *"I do."* Have you embraced the ministry for which you were created and are beginning? *"I have."*

TO THE BRIDE AND GROOM - Ceremonial Celebrant

By the public profession of your faith, be it known to all present that Jesus Christ of Nazareth is your personal Lord and Savior. I make this announcement before this congregation for two reasons. First, the bible declares that every person who confesses Christ before men will also be confessed by Jesus before God the Father. In the same respect, any person that denies Christ before others will also be denied by Jesus unto the Heavenly Father. And second, to allow others the opportunity to accept the redemption of Calvary and to receive the atoning salvation of Jesus Christ! Amen!

When two people join themselves to the Lord Jesus Christ by faith, according to the Written Word and preached gospel, they are cleansed by the shed blood of The Only Begotten Son. Because of the pure, holy and living blood of Jesus, this couple is purged and purified, and exist in the nature of glory even as Adam and Eve did in the Garden of Eden before their transgression. Their spirits have become renewed through Christ, for old things have passed away and all things are made new.

(Bride and Groom), a miracle took place at the exact moment you made Jesus the Lord of your life. Instantaneously, you were translated out of the domain of darkness into the kingdom of glorious light through the spiritual process of salvation. As a result, the sin nature that was abiding within you was completely abolished and replaced with the glorified nature of the Anointed One. This occurred as the Holy Ghost entered your lifeless spirit through the channel of your heart. At that moment, God's supernatural creative power caused your spirit to be reborn, which fulfilled the command of Jesus to *"be born again."*

God the Father used the same power source that raised His Son from the grave and delivered Him out of the grasp of sin, death and satan, to revitalize and rejuvenate your human spirit. All of this and so much more took place when you accepted Jesus as your personal Savior. Additionally, the instant you confessed your sin and professed Him as Lord of all, you were joined to Christ in the realm of the spirit and were simultaneously baptized into His corporate body as an individual member. As a result of your decision, you surrendered your life and no longer belong to yourself. From that moment onward, you became the private property of Jesus, because you were purchased with the price of His blood. All that He has is now yours, and all that you have is His. And together, as joint heirs, the two of you are one **WITH HIM** and one **IN HIM!!** Amen!

It is imperative that you comprehend and rightly discern the miracle that transpires in marriage. As new testament saints, your individual, glorified human spirits will be joined together to form a new spiritual entity. Two separate and distinct spirits will be jointly merged and ultimately re-emerge as a brand new spirit being. The creative dunamis of God will link, integrate and endlessly fuse you together as one creature. For the same power that initially united you to Jesus will also join you to each other forever! Halleluia!

It is essential that you realize that this uniting also includes **the consolidation of ethereal endowments!** For as you are spiritually combined, you will also be SYNCHRONOUSLY INTERWOVEN in spiritual gifts, ENTWINED in God- given abilities and HARMONIZED in the anointing! So be it! The grace, miraculous power and divine virtue of God will be COMPILED in this new creation as you become CONGRUOUS with The Christ. This culmination of spiritual attributes and qualities is awarded by God only in the covenant of marriage TO USE in life and the course of ministry.

Solomon revealed by divine inspiration that *"two are better than one."* He was unequivocally correct! I declare to you by the same Spirit that two human beings, unified as one in DUTY, PURPOSE AND GOD, releases the power of **INVINCIBILITY!!** I decree this day that the miraculous union of *(Bride and Groom)* will be eternally established upon the revelation of Jesus Christ and the person of the Holy Ghost, who is the Dynamic of Divine Dunamis!!! This preterhuman power will be discharged in daily life and ministry through the supernatural weapon of love. For the omnipotence of God is **released by** and **hidden in** the infinite love of God that is abundantly shed abroad in your hearts by the Holy Ghost. God's perfect love is the origin of your spiritual covenant and the source of your ministerial strength. It shall remain as the basis of your relationship for the rest of your human lives. For charity never fails. And the greatest of these is love. God's love. Agape love. And perfect love! Amen!

VOWS TO WITNESSES - Ceremonial Celebrant

TO THE CONGREGATION OF WITNESSES - Ceremonial Celebrant

I want to address the witnesses here. Jesus said in Matthew 18:19, *"That if TWO of you shall AGREE ON EARTH as touching anything that they shall ask, IT SHALL BE DONE FOR THEM of my Father which is in heaven."* As an ordained minister of God, who knows this couple and undoubtedly approves of this union, I touch and agree with *(Bride and Groom)* for their marriage. At this time, let the company of witnesses in attendance also acknowledge, correspond and agree with us for this consolidation to be done on the earth and in heaven in accordance with the perfect will of God. Be in one accord with me in asking the Heavenly Father for the miraculous union of *(Bride and Groom)* to come to pass now and forever.

In the eyes of the Supreme Being, these two individuals are washed in the precious blood of Jesus Christ, the Lamb of God. Their sins have been entirely removed, abolished and separated from them as far as the east is from the west. (Bride and Groom) are completely absolved from all wrongdoing and shortcoming, and are now at one with their Creator. They have prayed and diligently sought the face of the Lord about their mate in accordance with heaven's will and timing. This couple knows with all their heart that it is the perfect will of God for them to be joined together for a lifetime of caring, sharing and endless love together with a ministry of life, hope and purity in the Spirit of Christ.

They have made their decision in accordance with divine destiny and planned providence to remain one from now until the end of this dispensation. I charge this congregation as a minister of the Living God, who lays the proper foundation for this marriage and ministry, to do everything in your spiritual and natural power to nurture and cultivate this blessed union. See that it remains solidified, empowered, impassioned and flourishing in the Word and Spirit of God. For even as (Bride and Groom) are committed to each other's daily growth, so also I adjure thee to be dedicated to their progress, development and maturation.

Let not any family member, relation or stranger ever tamper, vex or speak against this agreement, for life and death are in the power of your tongue.

Regardless of what happens from this day forward, you must remain in a state of total agreement with this union because God's anointing of peace, compatibility of friendship and harmony of love abides within this twosome. The bible declares, *"Touch not my anointed, and do my prophets no harm."* DO NOT TOUCH *(Bride and Groom)* with your hands, minds or mouths! But rather, touch and agree with us for glory, victory and natural prosperity!! For whoever touches them, touches the apple of God's eye.

Woe and cursed be any individual or persons who would tamper with this anointed alliance to attempt its destruction, to annul its existence or cause it to be anything less than glorious in the eyes of King Jesus! No one can curse what God has blessed and none can reverse this anointed spoken benediction of grace. Amen! This marriage is a miraculous thing because it was determined and foreordained by God. And *"whatsoever is born of God overcomes the world."* This friendship, union and ministry was birthed by the Almighty and shall overcome all opposition, attacks, persecution, trials and tribulations of and in the world.

SERMON - *"The Miracle of Marriage"* - Ceremonial Celebrant - refer to pages 30-32.

PUBLIC PROFESSION OF VOWS - Ceremonial Celebrant

Since it is the agreement of *(Bride, Groom)*, myself, the five-fold officers present, and these witnesses for this twosome to be husband and wife, I ask that this couple would respond to these contractual obligations in the presence of God.

TO THE GROOM - Ceremonial Celebrant and Groom

(Full name of Groom), in most divine vow do you accept the bible as your foundation for spiritual guidance and enlightenment, as well as the basis of your total existence? *"Yes!"* Will you submit to its absolute authority, obey its commandments and do all that is written therein to the best of your ability by the grace of God? *"Yes!"* *(Full name of Groom)*, do you take this woman, who like Eve, was spiritually taken and placed beside you by God, to be your everlastingly wedded wife? *"I do!"* Do you earnestly vow before the Holy Trinity and those present that you will love her as Christ loved the church, and give yourself for her even to the extreme of physical death? *"I will!"* Will you die to yourself completely and live for Christ first and then *(name of Bride)* until death or the rapture shall separate you? *"I will!"* Will you daily obtain your fill of love from heaven's throne room and administer that anointing to *(Bride)* to continually perfect her? *"Yes, I will!"* As you grow and mature in God, will you also bless *(Bride)* with that increasing and intensifying agape love? *"Absolutely!"* Will you cover *(Bride)* with God's supernatural weapon of love because the anointing of agape covers a multitude of sins? *"I will!"* Will you sanctify, bless and continually cleanse her by washing her with the prophetic and written Word of God? *"I will."* Will you always appreciate and celebrate her? *"I will!"* To the extent that *(Bride)* will be presented to Jesus as a glorious member of His universal church, without natural spot or wrinkle, or any type of spoken defect? *"Yes, I will."* Will you perfect her in glory with the gifts and anointings given unto you so she will be holy and without utter blemish? *"I will."*

Will you love her as the wife of your youth, never despising her age or natural beauty, but spiritually nourish her and naturally cherish her as your own body? *"I will."* Will you love *(Bride)* in the same respect as your neighbor? *"I will."* Will you provide for her, comfort her, esteem her as the weaker vessel, honor her as a woman of virtue and heal her in time of sickness and debility? *"I will."* Will you fight for her and never let her die until the appointed time of her natural cessation? *"I will."* Will you forsake ALL other women on this earth and ALL manner of ungodly soulish relationship for *(Bride)* alone? *"Absolutely!"* Will you remain unswerving in your heart, fidel in your mind and uncorrupted in your eyes in respect to the lust of the flesh, the lust of the eyes and the pride of life this world offers? *"I will."* Will you abstain from all appearance of carnal and fleshly evil? *"I will."* Will you leave your father and mother and cleave to *(Bride)* as your wife? *"I will."* Will you perform unto her all the duties and obligations that a husband owes his wife as it is commanded in the holy writ? *"I will."* Will you remain absolutely faithful to God and *(Bride)* in spirit, soul and body, knowing this is well pleasing in the sight of your Creator? *"Yes!!"* Do you accept *(Bride)* as your natural help meet and spiritual miracle mate? *"I do."* Do you recognize your undisputed need for *(Bride)*, that she has gifts, talents and abilities that you need for the ministry you are beginning? *"Absolutely, I can't do it without her!"* Will you always keep her as your first ministry in accordance with the divine priorities of God? *"I will."*

TO THE BRIDE - Ceremonial Celebrant and Bride

(Full name of Bride), in most divine vow do you accept the bible as your foundation for spiritual guidance and enlightenment, as well as the basis of your total existence? *"Yes!"* Will you submit to its absolute authority, obey its every commandment and do all that is written therein to the best of your ability by the grace of God? *"Yes!"* *(Full name of Bride)*, do you take this man, from whose spiritual side you were created, to be your eternally wedded husband? *"I do."* Do you earnestly promise before all of the inhabitants of the third heaven and the earth, to love him unconditionally all the days of your life? *"I do."* Will you completely surrender to *(Groom)* in every area of your life: spirit, soul and body? *"I will."* Will you submit yourself to him in the same way you yield, surrender to and obey the Lord? *"I will."* Will you honor, esteem and respect your husband as your spiritual head and the appointed leader of this union, in accordance with the established divine order of God,

as he leads and governs in perfect love? *"I will."* As your husband, do you recognize and acknowledge that *(Groom)* represents Jesus Christ as the head of the church and the savior of His mortal body? *"I do."* Will you treat him in the same manner that you would personally minister to Jesus? *"I will."* Will you do him abundantly good and not evil all the days of his and your life? *"Yes, I will!"*

Will you remain subject unto your husband in everything, even as the church is subject unto Christ? *"Yes!"* Will you reverence *(Groom)* as a man of God, called to the governmental office of a (insert), and in all aspects of dutiful ministry? *"Yes!"* Will you walk in and administer the grace and mercy of God as he is perfected in that call and office? *"Yes, I will."* Will you always keep *(Groom)* as your first ministry in accordance with the divine priority of God? *"I will."* Will you die to yourself in all areas and live for *(Groom)* until death shall separate you? *"I will."* Will you exhort, edify and comfort *(Groom)* with the essence of the prophetic nature within? *"I will."* Will you honor him as a vessel of Righteousness that will be used by God in great power and glory? *"Absolutely!"* Will you overlook his shortcomings as he reaches for the prize of the high calling of God in Christ Jesus? *"I will."* Will you obey and follow him as he obeys the sublime prompting and leading of the Holy Spirit? *"Yes."* Do you acknowledge that God has ordained and equipped *(Groom)* to lead this Holy Union with the shepherd's staff and the rod of God! *"Yes, I do!"* Will you always remain faithful in word and deed to your husband and never speak death about him, to him or about your future relationship? *"I promise."* Will you remain unified with *(Groom)* to divide and conquer the enemy? *"Absolutely!"* Will you perform all the duties and responsibilities a wife is obligated by the bible to render unto her husband until death separates you? *"I will."*

PRESENTATION OF RINGS - Ceremonial Celebrant

The wedding ring is an outward and visible sign of the internal virtue and grace that spiritually joins a woman to a man. This ring signifies to all inhabitants in the spiritual and natural realm the betrothal, unifying and permanent bonding of *(Bride to Groom)* in holy matrimony by the supernatural power of the Holy Spirit.

TO GROOM: May I have the Bride's ring please.

TO BRIDE - Ceremonial Celebrant

This ring is an inestimable spiritual symbol. It is the tangible token of your faith, unswerving commitment and infinite love. This ring is fashioned of costly metal and contains many precious stones which reflect your jewel-like status before God. It is constructed in a never ending circle which signifies the undying continuum of God's perfect love, which is now manifest and shall be continually demonstrated in your relationship. And just as the circle has no beginning and no ending, the agape love of Almighty God is **infinitely limitless!** It encompasses eternity past and extends beyond the timeless future!! The love of God BEARS all things, BELIEVES all things, HOPES all things and ENDURES all things!!! **AND CHARITY NEVER FAILS!!!!** Amen!

Perfect love is the **driving force** of this union and the **binding power** of this covenant, because Jesus is the Lord of Love. He is the Master, Ruler and Governor of love. The **LOVE** of God and the **FAITH** of God are the spiritual dynamics that will cause God's miracle working power to exist in your lives and to be manifest in your ministry. **FOR FAITH WORKS BY LOVE AND LOVE WORKS MIRACLES!** HALLELUIA!

(Bride), God commands you to always wear this ring as a constant reminder of your faithful commitment, a continual announcement of the confession of your covenant to God and each other and an unchanging remembrance of your love contract. If anyone attempted to divide this union, it would be satan or a servant of the wicked one. This day, by the Spirit of God, I charge you to give no place to the devil and to be not ignorant of his devices. For this coupling, which occurs by the unction of the Holy Ghost, is

FOREVER! And the anointing of Almighty God always destroys the yoke of the devil! Amen!!

TO GROOM - Ceremonial Celebrant and Groom

(Groom), take this ring, place it on *(Bride's)* finger and make this profession of faith unto her: *"In token and covenental pledge of our unwavering faith in God, His Written Word and our enduring love for each other, with this ring I thee wed!! I, (Full name of Groom), according to the Word of God, leave my father and mother to join myself to you; to be your husband and the father of our children. From this moment forward, we shall be one in spirit, soul and body. This ring is an expression of my love for you, as well as an indication of my faith that I release now, in the name of the Father, Son and Holy Spirit! So it is spoken and so it is done!"*

TO BRIDE: May I have the Groom's ring please.

TO GROOM - Ceremonial Celebrant

A ring can mean two different things. It can be a never-ending sign of love or it can be a shackle of bondage and imprisonment. *(Groom)*, I charge you by the Spirit of the Living God, to always remember that this woman stands by your side. She is not above you and you are not above her. She is not below you and you are not below her. You are the same. For out of the SIDE of man was woman created. You are equal! Equally created, equally called, equally endowed and equal in ministry! Amen! *(Groom)*, you have been given the awesome responsibility of being the head of this union, to lead this relationship in love and guide it into God's glory. For you will go, grow and glow from glory to glory to glory! Halleluia!

As you wear this ring, always remember that *(Bride)* was bestowed unto you as a gift from God. She is your natural helpmate and your spiritual miracle mate. For God has supernaturally equipped her with abilities and anointings that are mandatory for what you are about to do. Never look upon this wedding ring as a shackle or a means of dominance. Always remember that *(Bride)* is an indispensable part of your life and an integral component of the supernatural provision that God has granted and imparted unto you.

TO BRIDE - Ceremonial Celebrant and Bride

(Bride), I want you to know that there is no place in the bible that gives one the right to dominate and subjugate another. Your vows have clearly stated that you will submit to each other in the fear of the Lord and in the responsibilities of this life, knowing that God's grace will make the difference. Take this ring, place it on *(Groom's)* finger and make this profession of faith unto him: *"In token and covenantal pledge of our unwavering faith in God, His Written Word and our enduring love for each other, with this ring, I thee wed!! I, (Full name of Bride), according to the Word of God, submit and surrender myself to you, to be your wife and the mother of our children. From this moment forward, we shall be one in spirit, soul and body. I know with all of my heart that this commitment is forever, and is as unchanging and endless as the love and faith of The Heavenly Father, His Son Jesus Christ and the Holy Ghost. So it is spoken and so it is done!"*

HONORING OF BRIDE & GROOM - Bride and Groom - refer to pages 33-37

LIGHTING OF THE UNITY CANDLE - Ceremonial Celebrant

As new testament believers, we exist on the earth to bear witness of the Light, that all men through the Spirit of God might believe and know Him. For Jesus Christ is *"the only true Light which lighteth every man that cometh into the world."* Jesus left His position with God in glory and came to this planet to send forth fire on the earth and to baptize His disciples with the Holy Ghost. As God incarnate, Jesus was immeasurably anointed by the Spirit of God. He blazed with the igneous nature of unquenchable fire and enkindled the course of this world. Jesus ignited the inhabitants of the earth, and activated His chosen followers for ministry and the continuation of the new covenant.

As present day disciples who abide in the light, splendor and glory of the Anointed One, we have been commissioned to inflame others with the fire of the Holy Spirit and the consuming temperament of God. And even as Jesus is the Light of the World, as ambassadors of Christ and appointed representatives of His kingdom, we likewise bear His illuminance because we are the brightness of Jesus' glory and the express image of His person. So, shine, Jesus, shine. Glow, Jesus, glow, in *(Bride and Groom)*. And grow in the radiant resplendence beyond the blue flambeau! Amen!!

I decree this day by the Holy Ghost that the fire in this relationship shall burn forever and never go out. The inward flame shall burn with greater intensity, energy and vehemence! The breath of the Lord like a stream of brimstone shall continually kindle you and your relationship. Your marriage shall blaze stronger, hotter and more fervent with an ever-increasing, consuming magnitude of fervor, zeal and passion. Jesus, I ask that the eyes of *(Bride and Groom)* glare with discernment as a flame of fire. Let their mouths blaze with your prophetic issue as a fiery stream. Let the brilliance of your Word guide them and the illuminance of your Spirit enlighten them with life changing Rhema revelation.

COMMUNION - Ceremonial Celebrant to Bride and Groom.

"Come and gather yourselves together unto the heavenly banquet of the great God." Please kneel to symbolically partake in the Marriage Supper of the Lamb.

As a result of your covenantal vows, the two of you now exist as a new spiritual identity. This is biblically confirmed, for when created humanity was united as male and female, God called their name Adam! Amen! Initially, when both of you were first born-again, you became new creatures in Christ. In your present and ceaseless state of togetherness, the two of you have again become new creatures in Christ because of your spiritual consolidation. <u>YOU ARE NOW ONE AND WILL ALWAYS BE ONE!!</u> Therefore, when you stand together in earthly matters and agree in kingdom business, you shall quickly behold the manifested result. For the **intersection** of two saints causes a great disturbance in the spirit realm, but the **integration** of two believers that are synthesized as **ONE** by the Holy Ghost, produces a cataclysmic reaction that releases tremendous transcendental power! IN REALITY, AS ONE AMALGAMATED SPIRIT, YOU BECOME A VIRTUAL, EFFECTUAL, DYNAMIC DUO!

This spiritual force unchannels the great grace and magnificent might that is on reserve and at your disposal because of the Law of the Power of Flight. Deuteronomy 32:30 reveals this spiritual statute for miraculous ministry for *"ONE can chase a THOUSAND, and TWO can put TEN THOUSAND to flight..."*. You will personally witness the manifestation of this power in your daily life and ministry as you continue to grow and mature. But from this moment on, your everyday life will be exponentially more powerful and your spiritual existence will reflect a power source 10,000 times as great!!

As believers, both of you have partaken and received the supernatural substance of the communion table. You understand the spiritual significance of participating in the body and blood of Christ and the importance of its regular consumption. The covenant of communion was **initiated** at the last supper, **ratified** by the shed blood of Jesus at Calvary and shall be shortly **consummated** at the forthcoming Marriage Supper of the Lamb! It is imperative in these first moments of your new spiritual existence that you supernaturally seal your union by partaking in the table of the Lord. In Matthew 26:26, as the Master and His disciples ate the passover, *"Jesus took*

BREAD, and BLESSED it, and BRAKE it, and gave it to the disciples, and said, Take, eat; THIS IS MY BODY."

Jesus took bread and blessed it. The bread symbolized His body in the spirit realm. In the process of blessing, Jesus actually anointed His entire spiritual body through this prophetic benediction of grace. God the Father blessed the flesh and blood of His Son before it was broken to nullify all fleshly and demonic curses originally instituted in the third chapter of Genesis. This was first done spiritually and then fulfilled naturally. The human body of Jesus bore 39 physical lacerations, which fulfilled the curse of the law utilized by demonic forces to empower sin, sickness and natural death! By these stripes, God prepared and supplied the provision for all believers to appropriate **TOTAL PHYSICAL HEALING!** The natural body of Jesus was stricken, smitten and afflicted for our spiritual transgressions, iniquities and shortcomings. We now live in health, wholeness and complete bodily soundness because of His bruised, wounded and broken body! Glory to God! As you eat and consume the blessed flesh of His Person, accept and receive the spiritual and natural nourishment necessary to sustain your human bodies and withstand all physical malady!

GIVE BODY TO NEWLYWEDS - Ceremonial Celebrant

It is written in Leviticus 17:11 that *"the life of the flesh is in the blood."* Originally, blood was utilized in the sacrificial offering of the high priest to make atonement for the body and soul of God's people because the blood contained the life of the living being. As this truth is applied to the communion table of the new covenant, it reveals that the blood of Jesus Christ embodies the spiritual life of God Himself! This means that the life of the glorified flesh of the Son of God is inherent in the blood of Jesus!! Therefore, the blood of Jesus the Savior that exists within a born-again believer through ingestion and digestion, bears the very life of the Almighty!!! This consists of the undying, everlasting and divine life of the Supreme Being of the Universe!! Praise God!!!!

After Jesus gave bread to the disciples *"he took the cup, and gave thanks, and gave it to them saying, Drink ye all of it, FOR THIS IS MY BLOOD of the new testament, which is shed for many for the remission of sin."* The shed blood of Jesus Christ sanctions the new covenant, cleanses man from all sin and is the anointed actuant applied for atoning salvation! We drink the blood of Jesus in glorious remembrance of His total victory over satan, to receive the spiritual sustenance of immortality, to purge the body and soul of sin and in heavenly preparation for the approaching Marriage Supper of the Lamb! Jesus referred to this great festive celebration in Matthew 26:29 when He declared, *"I will not drink henceforth of this fruit of the vine, until THE DAY when I drink it NEW WITH YOU IN MY FATHER'S KINGDOM."* Only at this great heavenly banquet will the new covenant of Jesus Christ be finally fulfilled forever!!

This day, as you drink of the cup of the vine, remember the work of the cross, appropriate its perfect atonement and anticipate the Marriage Supper of the Lamb. For in the body and blood of Jesus Christ is the preternatural provision for the total human being: spirit, soul and body! Abide and continue in the zoe life of this prepared provision, and be spiritually and naturally strengthened by the vitality and endless energy of His Body and Blood. Eat, drink and live in continual remembrance of the broken body and shed blood of the Lord Jesus Christ.

GIVE BLOOD TO NEWLYWEDS - Ceremonial Celebrant to Bride and Groom

Together, the two of you have been invested with the God-given authority and power to rebuke, repel and return all natural disease and soulish disorder designed, devised and dispatched by the demons of hell. The Spirit of God says, *"Always exercise this authority and spiritual right."*

PRONOUNCEMENT OF HOLY UNION - Ceremonial Celebrant

TO BRIDE, GROOM AND ALL PRESENT

The Godhead has solemnized this union of one. Therefore, this anointed alliance will NEVER be defiled or dissolved for ANY reason! For this everlasting covenant of marriage is honored, consecrated and sanctified by the Triune Being! **IT IS FINISHED!!** As a five-fold representative of Jesus Christ, before Almighty God and in the name of the Father, His Son Jesus Christ and by the omnipotent power of the Holy Spirit of the Living God, I now pronounce you one. You are now and forever, husband and wife. You may seal your covenant by kissing the bride.

ANOINTING AND BLESSING OF THE UNION - Ceremonial Celebrant

Please remain kneeling for the duration of prophetic presbytery. Galatians 3:13 reveals that Christ redeemed us from the curse of the law by becoming every curse for us, so that the bountiful blessings of Abraham might come upon all believers through Jesus. You must realize that God has blessed you with all spiritual blessings in heavenly places in Christ Jesus. **BELIEVE** and **RECEIVE** this furnished grace today for the rest of your lives! Accept these supernatural privileges for your spiritual advantage and natural benefit!

At this time, I am going to decree your spiritual and natural blessings, and God will bestow His abounding grace upon *(Bride and Groom)*. Remember, your acceptance and receipt of the Holy Ghost is only the earnest of your heavenly inheritance! According to Deuteronomy 28, all of these blessings will come on you and abundantly overtake you as you hearken unto the voice of the Lord your God.

"Blessed shalt thou be in the city, and blessed shalt thou be in the field. Blessed shall be the fruit of thy body, and the fruit of thy ground, and the fruit of thy cattle, the increase of thy kine, and the flocks of thy sheep. Blessed shall be thy basket and thy store. Blessed shalt thou be when thou comest in, and blessed shalt thou be when thou goest out. The Lord shall cause thine enemies that rise up against thee to be smitten before thy face: they shall come out against thee one way, and flee before thee seven ways. The Lord shall command the blessing upon thee in thy storehouses, and in all that thou settest thine hand unto; and he shall be thee in the land which the Lord thy God giveth thee. The Lord shall establish thee an holy people unto himself, as he hath sworn unto thee, if thou shalt keep the commandments of the Lord thy God, and walk in his ways. And all people of the earth shall see that thou art called by the name of the Lord; and they shall be afraid of thee.

And the Lord shall make thee plenteous in goods, in the fruit of thy body, and in the fruit of thy cattle, and in the fruit of thy ground, in the land which the Lord sware unto thy fathers to give thee. The Lord shall open unto thee his good treasure, the heaven to give the rain unto thy land in his season, and to bless all the work of thine hand: and thou shalt lend unto many nations, and thou shalt not borrow. And the Lord shall make thee the head, and not the tail; and thou shalt be above only, and thou shalt not be beneath; if that thou hearken unto the commandments of the Lord thy God, which I command thee this day, to observe and to do them."

PROPHETIC PRESBYTERY TO BRIDE & GROOM - Ceremonial Celebrant and other invited ministers.

PROPHETIC PRESBYTERY TO IMMEDIATE FAMILIES - Ceremonial Celebrant and other invited ministers.

PRESENTATION OF NEWLYWEDS TO THE CONGREGATION OF WITNESSES

(Bride & Groom), please turn and face the congregation. Ladies and gentlemen, for the first time in human history, it is a great honor to introduce to you, Mr. & Mrs. *(insert first name, middle initial and last name of Groom)*. **"WHAT GOD HAS PUT TOGETHER, NO ONE WILL PUT ASUNDER."**

THE SERMON - *"THE MIRACLE OF MARRIAGE"* - Ceremonial Celebrant

Most are somewhat familiar with the ceremony of marriage. But a majority are ignorant of what actually occurs between two born-again, spirit-filled believers. I am referring to the UNIFICATION OF THE GLORIFIED NATURE OF MAN AND WOMAN in marriage. Specifically, the joining of the contents of their spirits which consists of **GODLY GIFTS, GRACE AND GLORY!** Within the spirit being of saints exist separate and distinct gifts that are individually given to men and women. God will bestow associated anointings and related spiritual endowments to persons destined for marriage. Analogous, coinciding and corresponding divine gratuities are granted by God unto husband and wife for ministry. This is especially true in the emphasis of TEAM MINISTRY, where the gifts are complementary.

1 Corinthians 12:1 *"Now concerning spiritual gifts, brethren, I would not have you ignorant."* The Greek for *"ignorant"* is *"agnoeo"* = not to know through lack of information or intelligence; or to ignore through disinclination. Gifts are spiritual tools delegated and consigned by God to establish and build His kingdom on the earth.

1 Corinthians 12:4 *"Now there are diversities of gifts, but the same Spirit."* The Greek for *"diversities"* is *"diairesis"* = a distinction, difference or variety. The Greek for *"gifts"* is *"charisma"* = a divine gratuity, a spiritual endowment or a miraculous faculty. The HOLY GHOST solely distributes unique divine gratuities, extraordinary spiritual endowments and awe-inspiring miraculous faculties!! Not only are there diversities of gifts but also a variety of administrations, operations and manifestations. The same Triune Being consisting of God the Father, the Lord Jesus Christ and the Holy Spirit, works them unanimously! One in one and all in all!

1 Corinthians 12:7 *"But the manifestation of the Spirit is given to every man to profit withal."* The intent and objective of the endowment is **SPIRITUAL PROFIT.** Gifts are given to be used in conjunction with divine will for the spiritual advancement of the body of Christ - Kingdom profit = People profit!! Miraculous faculties are bestowed by the Holy Spirit for testimonial confirmation: for public demonstration, exhibition and manifestation **in word and deed.** Gifts are given by the Spirit to manifest God's Greatness - Miracles = THE GLORY OF GOD! Amen!

1 Corinthians 12:8 *"For to one is given by the Spirit the word of wisdom; to another the word of knowledge by the same Spirit; To another faith by the same Spirit; to another the gifts of healings by the same Spirit; To another the working of miracles; to another prophecy; to another discerning of spirits; to another divers kinds of tongues; to another the interpretation of tongues."*

Utterance gifts, power gifts and other gifts are all divinely granted by the **GRACE** of God. They are selected and obtained from the complete spiritual mantle that Jesus sustained as the full extent of the Holy Ghost. This is confirmed in John 3:34 for *"God giveth not the Spirit by measure unto him."* The Greek for *"giveth not"* = giveth. The Greek phrase *"by measure"* means a limited degree or portion = FULL MEASURE!! Jesus operated in the full measure of the Spirit in ministry. As believers, we also can partake in this divine ability and receive immeasurable portions of the mantle of glory Jesus operated under and ministered with as the Son of Man. This initially occurred *"when he ascended up on high, and led captivity captive..."*. At that time, Jesus *"gave gifts unto men."* The Greek for *"gifts"* is *"doma"* = a present or gift. Jesus gave gifts unto all wanting and anticipating believers on the earth from the unlimited extent of His spiritual mantle. Today, the Holy Ghost is responsible for the division, distribution and operation of these spiritual endowments.

1 Corinthians 12:11 *"But all these worketh that one and selfsame Spirit, dividing to every man severally as he will."* The gifts are divided severally by the will of the Holy Ghost. Severally = many, numerous and an abundance. Severally to one and severally to another. Numerous gifts to husband and numerous gifts to wife! Gifts are divided and separated for specific ministry and classified by individual call!! And two like calls will receive similar spiritual gifts!!!

Romans 12:6 *"Having then GIFTS DIFFERING ACCORDING TO THE GRACE that is given to us..."* Grace is freely given and to be freely received! There are DIVERSITIES OF GRACE IN HUSBAND AND WIFE. The GRACE OF GOD determines the GIFTS OPERATIVE IN TEAM MINISTRY.

When this truth is applied to marital ministry it means that **EITHER SPOUSE HAS THE LEGAL LICENSE AND SPIRITUAL AUTHORITY TO OPERATE IN THE GIFTS AND ANOINTINGS OF THEIR MATE,** as long as they remain submitted to their partner and the Spirit of God! Why? Because in marriage, THE TWO ARE ONE! Consequently, they are permitted to operate in any miraculous faculty that exists in the new unified spiritual creation under command or by divine directive. Why? Because the combined gifts of God are now a part of their united glorified nature and spiritual identity. The gracious gratuities were bestowed unto each other through their partner in marriage.

1 Peter 4:10-11 *"As every man hath **RECEIVED THE GIFT**, even **SO MINISTER** the same one to another, as good stewards of the manifold grace of God."* Gifts of grace are provided and received to serve, care for and to minister unto others. And the spirit of glory is ever present in God's manifold grace. His glory is within, upon and flows out of the unctuous union.

The glory of THE MIRACLE OF MARRIAGE is that two equivalent calls IN A PREDETERMINED MARRIAGE receive a culmination of miraculous faculties to operate as <u>AN AUTONOMOUS ALLIANCE</u>! Halleluia! The Holy Ghost always aids, assists and allocates ALL ANOINTING that is needed in that union for ministry! In the sacrament of marriage, the gifts that were once divided are then reassembled and compiled in the new spirit being of the husband and wife. What was once DIVIDED and INDIVIDUAL is then ADDED and AMASSED for COMPLETE HARMONY AND SPIRITUAL SYNERGISM! Glory!

As a result, the power of God is multiplied exponentially in marriage for the express purpose of victorious and overcoming ministry! All spiritual gifting is unremittingly deposited in the combined, whole and aggregated being of the new spiritual creature. In THE MIRACLE OF MARRIAGE, the joining of spirits automatically fuses the spiritual gifts in the glorious new entity! Why? To fulfill, complement and perfect EACH OTHER, and THOSE WHO WILL RECEIVE FROM THEIR HAND OF MINISTRY. In THE MIRACLE OF MARRIAGE, there is not just an intersecting of two distinct spirits, but a complete unification and consolidation of glorified spirit including innate gifting.

THE HONORING OF BILL PANKO - Margaret Panko

My beloved William! I greatly appreciate and honor you this day as my husband, my man and my man of God! The name *"William"* is derived from two Latin words *"will"* and *"helm"* which are combined to mean willingness to protect. For me, your name proclaims my man will protect me from harm, sickness and all the evil influences of the devil! For you are my earthly protector and God in you is my spiritual and natural shelter!! Amen! You were provided in my life as a strong pillar, so I could lean on you in times of help and need. And at <u>ALL</u> times, I find great rest and peace in your arms. For where you are there is home! And how I love, when you are near! Never fear dear, for I will never leave thee nor depart from our home!

Sweetheart, your presence in my life makes me more special and beautiful each and every day. And for this reason, I will make you even more wonderful than you already are! Because you spiritually cover and comfort me, I will now do the same. Today and forever, you will wear the vestment of virtue which has been dipped in the blood of the Lamb. And the crimson stains of your former life and this present world are now thoroughly cleansed and made as white as snow. This day you stand before your Creator pure, fresh and new! (**Margaret puts the Robe of Righteousness on Bill**) Now, you are fit for royalty with the robe of His Majesty! (**Margaret places a sovereign crown on Bill's head**) And now you are ready for the coronation of this world and the next. For the time has come for the ordination of the kingly company of prophets and high priests. Honey, today, between you, me and the Trinity, the Marriage Supper of the Lamb is come.

It will be a great delight to tend, serve and care for you all the days of my life. For as I love you with God's agape love, I am actually loving Jesus my Savior, because you represent the Lord in our marriage. And I will honor and respect you in the same manner that I revere the King of Kings and the Lord of Lords. You shall be my little lord. Not my Savior, for **NO ONE** can take the place of Jesus in my life! But, my lord and my earthly husband, as a man of great spiritual authority and power. For even as Sarah called Abraham *"lord"* with a small L, so also I call you *"lord"* with a small L.

God has given you to me for just a short period of time. And even as we become one this day, you are not really mine. You have only been loaned unto me for a season, for the days of our lives and the extent of our earthen ministry. For it is Jesus who bought you, owns you and whom you live for! You have only been temporarily bestowed unto me as an imperial gift from His Excellency.

Bill, you have kept your eyes on the Lord and on me for 7 years, and 7 is the number of completion. This day I complete you naturally as your **help meet** and complement you spiritually as your **miracle mate!** And in the year of eight, ALL will be great! For no longer will I just be your date, but your eternal help mate! Amen!

I thank the Heavenly Father that you're not like any other man. There is not another living creature on this earth that can compare with you. Your visible zeal, passion and intensity truly makes you one in five billion! And you are a great guy because you serve a **GREAT GOD!** You have desired to see and will experience the great things and movements of God because God is in you in a big way. This has even been confirmed in personal prophecy for God said, *"You have a heart for big things because I'm a big God and I'm a big God in you."* 100% Perfect healing and the realm of *"greater works"* are your spiritual destiny. For God will be greater than what you've KNOWN, greater than what you BELIEVED FOR and greater than what you EXPECTED! The ministry we are called to will be exceedingly abundant above all that we could ever ask or think!!

Bill, you are the type of man who is willing to work hard and forego everything to get the real. To know the truth, the real truth and the revelational truth that sets you and others free. Daily you dig deep to obtain and secure the genuine gospel straight from the Source. For God first reveals things unto His prophets. And God will consume you. He will put His word in your mouth and it will come forth with fluidity and accuracy. It will be a prophetic word, a word with insight, a word with revelation, a word with foresight and a word with instant inspiration! For revelation knowledge and a spontaneous utterance will come forth as you minister under God's prophetic mantle.

I realize you thrive on life changing revelation and know you will live the remainder of your total natural existence on the cutting edge of the Spirit. For you will receive thoughts from God and you will write about the present, the distant future and dispensations thousands of years from now! Great revelation will flow from the mind of the Holy Ghost, to your spirit, to your pen, to paper and ultimately to the nations! Amen! In the millennium and ages to come, your great grandchildren will read about you. They will study your Godly character and emulate the man of strength you are becoming. They will work the miracles you work and marvel at what God has accomplished through you.

You know, the Lord showed me in a vision that you were walking with a flag. And that flag represented something. It represented freedom. It was the **FLAG OF FREEDOM!** As you carry this flag in the days to come, God is going to move mighty. God is going to move mighty because He has equipped you with the shepherd's staff to lead the people of God. And you will shepherd many people in the house of the Lord as you <u>GOVERN GOD'S GLORY!</u>

Sweetie, together, just you and me, we will make our hearts, souls and lives sing. Just you and me! NO ONE ELSE will come nigh you, or come nigh me! Now and forever, IT'S JUST YOU AND ME! And that makes me very happy! For **OUR KING** has intervened!! And as He continues to intercede, we will go, grow and glow from glory to glory. Bill, you're a thrill and you're the Lord's will. You are as precious as the Rose of Sharon, and more fresh and pleasing than the fragrance of the morning dew. And I will **ALWAYS** love you!! You are altogether lovely! You are my beloved!! And you are my best friend!!!

THE HONORING OF MARGARET PANKO - Bill Panko

The name *"Margaret"* means a pearl and a gift of God, and this is exactly what you are to God and me. A jewel, a gem and a magnificent treasure bestowed unto me by your Creator. This was even confirmed in personal prophecy, for God spoke to you and said, *"I'm excited about your future and your walk with me. I'm just filled with joy over you. You're just like a TROPHY to me. You're just like a **JEWEL** to me. I'm making you out of GOLD, and when I'm done, I'm going to pour My glory through you!"* Margaret, you are a modern day present in the form of a person who possesses attributes, qualities and traits that today's women do not have. For you are a beauty of the SKIN and a beauty of the SPIRIT! Amen!

I thank God for your unfeigned spiritual support and patronage in my life. This backing originates from the gifting within you which is the true prophetic nature of Christ. For the gift of exhortation, edification and comfort flows naturally from your heart and the core of your being! Halleluia! This day, I enter into a **PROPHETIC PARTNERSHIP** with you! We shall be an unctuous union and an anointed alliance, incorporated by Christ and merged together in marriage, for the mutual manifestation of miracles. Ours will be a PROPHETIC MARRIAGE! For I have been divinely called to be a prophet and a prophetic businessman, and you a prophetess and a prophetic psalmist.

In ministry, you and I will flow together in <u>THE UNLIMITED POTENCY OF DECREED DOMINION!</u> As a prophetic pair, we shall overcome ALL and victory will be our portion!! As God continues to open the prophetic flow, I will hearken unto the Holy Ghost in you and through you, for you will speak as a voice for God and your tongue shall preach the gospel. A PROPHETIC HERITAGE is our divine destiny, for it has been revealed that within our seed is a mighty generation! Margaret, you are a tremendous **addition** to me, the **complete** complement and **perfect** supplement! Next to Jesus, you are the biggest blessing in my life!

The perfect agape love that resides within you endlessly emanates from the infinite depths of your being. Your empathetic nature and tenderhearted disposition are your greatest gifts because they genuinely represent Jesus Christ. And the ANOINTING OF LOVE in your life, induces the MANTLE OF COMPASSION, which arouses the internal charity to help the afflicted, grieved and tormented. You respond to the hurting and neglected by REACHING OUT to make all better. And upon contact, the power of God is discharged through **THE LOVE TOUCH,** to heal and set the captives free! Your entire lifetime will be spent ministering this most precious sought after gift to a dying and desperately needing world, for this was the purpose of your creation.

Margaret, not only do I honor you as a virtuous woman, but I also esteem you as a woman of great virtue and power. As a true servant and woman of God called to be a prophetess, you possess the compassion of Christ that generates an endless supply of supernatural power, which manifests **miracles in word and deed!** The mantle of compassion upon you and the gift of mercy within you will unleash the unlimited potentate of the Trinity. God verified this truth by the mouth of His servant as He declared, *"This will also be the time where you're going to FIND that the **SUBSTANCE AND ABUNDANCE** that you have desired, is going to be in your hands. The WEAPONS are going to be in your hands. The TOOLS are going to be in your hands. **ALL** that is needed, you're going to FIND that IT IS ALREADY THERE IN PRESENT."* Margaret, God commands you to **"USE IT"!!!**

In my entire lifetime, I have never met anyone who honors, esteems and values the gift of life more than you. You acknowledge human life as God's most precious, priceless possession and earthly endowment. Sweetheart, you overtly demonstrate a zeal for living that can not be measured or matched! Truly, you have been smeared with the **oil of joy** and the **anointing of gladness**, which will continually energize your total being with the strength of the Lord, to overcome all opposition and obstacles in the world.

Margaret, you are my beloved best friend and cherished Christian confidant, and I honor you this day as my bride! I praise and thank the Heavenly Father for creating you and bestowing you unto me. I am forever excited about us, and that today, you will finally be my help meet and miracle mate!! Margaret, you and I deserve the best, that's why we have each other, and that's why God brought us together!!! Honey, truly, you are blessed and truly, you're the best! God's best!! And my best!!! So it is now and so it shall be forever!!!!

DOWNTOWN CAMPUS LRC

J. SARGEANT REYNOLDS COMMUNITY COLLEGE
3 7219 00111297 1

```
HQ 745 .P3 1993
Panko, Bill.
The miracle of marriage
```

DISCARDED

J. SARGEANT REYNOLDS COMMUNITY COLLEGE
Richmond, VA